SOUL CLAIMING

Jody Aliesan   (photo: Michael Katz)

SOUL CLAIMING

poems by
Jody Aliesan

drawings by
Julie King

MULCH  PRESS

a haystack book

Many of these poems first appeared in the following magazines: *Aphra, Everywoman, The Higginson Journal of American Poetry, Images, Isthmus, KRAB Program Guide, Moving Out, Northwest Passage, Pandora, Portland Review, Puget Soundings, Rough Times, Signpost, The Texas Slough, Women: A Journal of Liberation,* and *WomanSpirit.* Several poems were first published in *Thunder in the Sun* (University of Washington YWCA, 1971) and *To Set Free* (Second Moon, 1972).

Special thanks to Dena Dawson and David Dawson, who fed my spirit and pruned my words

and to the women of Pandora, who for five years have given my work a home.

Mulch Press would like to acknowledge the assistance of The National Endowment for the Arts and The Coordinating Council of Literary Magazines which helped make the publication of this book possible.

Mulch Press   *New York Office:*
P.O. Box 598   326A Fourth St.
Northampton, Mass. 01060   Brooklyn, N.Y. 11215

CONTENTS

DRAWINGS by Julie King appear on pp. *x, 6, 9, 20, 24, 29, 40, 48, 53,* and *65.*

for Randy

Coal and Silver

julie king

Coal and Silver

Snow blows in front of the streetlights
in all directions,
pulls veils down over the evergreens.
Tomato vines and sunflower leaves
are black with cold.

> My spirit catcher is the deer.
> My ally is the rope plant
> and my protector is the moon.
> She turns me into a pine tree
> and strews mushrooms at my feet.
> I see an owl on her shoulder,
> a cup in her hand.

Time for gathering up the dead
cucumber leaves and summer squash,
marigolds, nasturtiums,
into the hot belly of compost heap—
earth pregnant with another year.

> I have a ring of magic stones
> (blue green yellow orange),
> I am afraid of closed places:
> (black white purple red)
> tombs, cells, hospital rooms,
> stairwells, coffins, closets, caves,
> the inside of my head,
> the small bleeding pear between my eggs.

The days leave earlier.
Now my shovel scrapes after nightfall.

> My omens are butterflies and birds.
> Crabs scuttle in my gut.

She had lived by the river long enough
that she could remember how it used to sound—
once it was in sheets hissing cold over the rocks
and now low comfortable lapping, slapping,
or honey ripples lolling in the even sun.
She knew its syllables below the water flow,
could tell you in darkness which stones were speaking,
when the upcountry snow had all melted,
read season change in foampatch bubbles.
Once she could walk downstream at midnight
and know from the echoes
how far she had gone.

Waiting

Winter is shorter when you know a garden
and can still pull beets in early December.
Even after everything's turned under
long nights are hours of rest, not death,
earned sleep after the land's labor

when kitchen tables bear seed packets,
almanacs, sketches,
when conversation
conjures up a tangled trellis of peas
before the first one plumps up in a furrow.

That day apple twigs are already knobbier,
crocus tips slice old mulch,
                February
is already spring.

Robins watch the hoe.

Rain in October:
already
I smell winter.
House lights on the hill
poke star points
through the door screen.
Too wet today
for painting the fence.
A good night for soup,
books in the rocking chair.

I smell winter,
I'm glad for it.
I'm ready to finish,
fall ripe off the tree,
crawl into my lair.
I'm nearly deaf
from the buzz of things growing.
We all need some death
to prune us back,
slow us down.

The room will stay warm
if I close all the curtains.
It won't be long
before I'll need
      another blanket
      hot cranberry juice
      the trunk full of sweaters.
It'll feel clean to be cold
burrowing down
under the year.

Ancient Race

It would serve us right
if some morning we woke up
and they were in control again,
buckling the sidewalks
rising up through the freeway
wading into the lakes
prying open the windows.

We bind their roots with clay,
far from the jungles,
order them into rows for our harvest.
They live if we remember,
die without a sound.

Our species is so advanced
we have to tape wires to them,
cut them up with scissors
to believe they can feel.

Each night we walk through houses
in every window we see them
sitting on the sill,
standing near the glass
as if waiting for a signal.

Julie King

I. Copper Ridge

From our bed
on Lookout Mountain
near the snowmelt, on a patch
of scrubby heather
we could fall three thousand feet
into the faint roar of the Chilliwak,
into the fir-lined jaws of the dark valley.
Around us, a stormy sea of stone
lifts whitecaps without sound or motion
under the blue searchlight of the moon.
We know their names,
we watched them spring from topo lines
as we switchbacked up,
we might reach across and stroke their glaciers
some other time.
There is not one cloud on the star-dome.
There is too much magic for sleeping.
Already far past where we can count them
a few granite breakers shine with the morning;
below us on the wind a hawk stops,
falls like a stone into the canyon.

II. Song for Randy

Blueberry huckleberry
thimbleberry sprout
wild mountain sorrel
and three fat trout.
One slipped off the hook
catch it if you can
so big it must be cut in two
to fit the frying pan.
The fifteen inch for you
the fourteen inch for me
the third we'll have for breakfast
with a cup of yarrow tea.

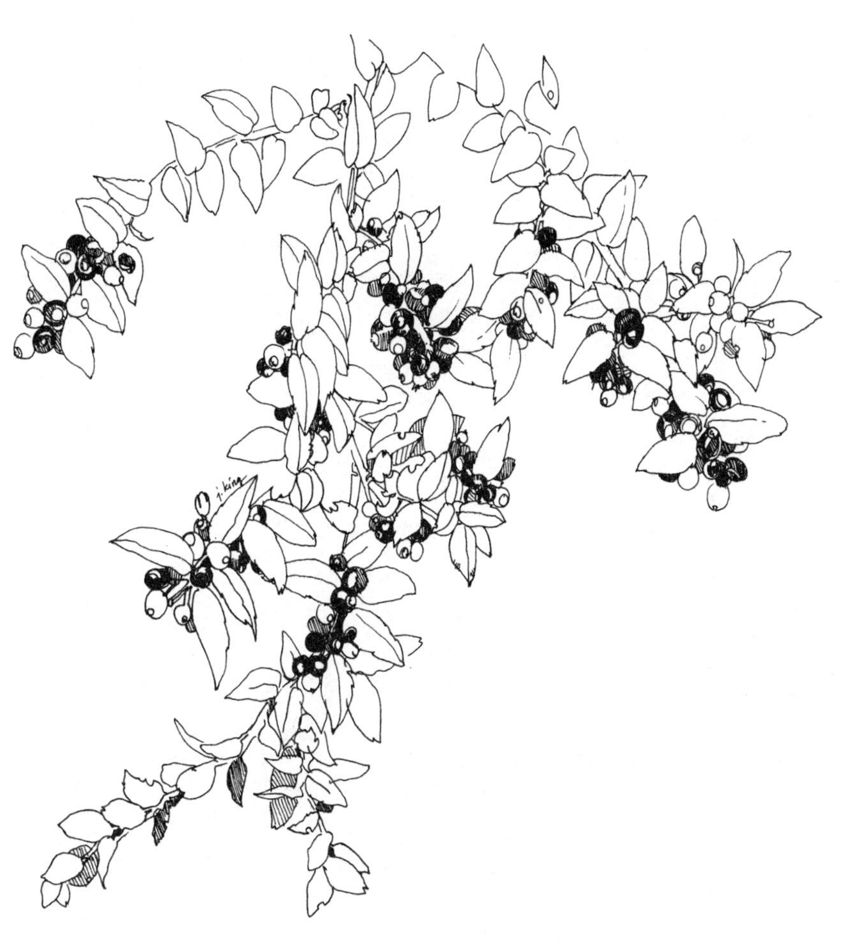

III. Abandoned trail

Twinflowers and coolwort grow in the path.
Moss and fern nearly carpet the way.
A season's scattering of hemlock cones
lies undisturbed,
crisp under our steps.

No crushing feet have passed here for some time
except down by the stream
where the bears drink
watching the log bridge rot.

Sawtooth Mountains

I. Looking eastward

Between the sundown and the full moon's rising
I feel the earth move
so slowly not even the high trees know
but steadily, with much practice
rolling me and where I lie into its shadow.
Stars fastening along the ridge
push off to float where the Dippers turn.
Meteors like random spinning lures
drag without a ripple through dark pools
and I pull my own hooks across deep places
searching for old, calm thoughts.
They surface rippling here and there, fish rising.

II. Divide

Only walkers reach these places.
High country humbles wheels
and horses have trouble scrambling on the rocks.
Maybe a helicopter
could hover down stone walls
(I don't know about helicopters)
but it wouldn't be the same as standing here
where everything begins.
No sound except new water from the snow
and wind strumming the granite minarets.
Nothing grows but lichen and scrub grass,
the sky, and wordless spaces in my soul.
Native peoples know the way to be:
you must carry as little as you can
and go by foot to reach a sacred place.

Fate, blocking and carrying me
is a deep signal from my own cells:
genes lined up on a chromosome,
twisted tapes of chemicals,
which are, finally, carbon atoms,
nucleus, electrons,
and these not particles, but vibrations
clouding together as galaxies
on both ends of this telescope.

> The fiddling physicist
> allowed as how
> there's no way to know
> how fast we're going,
> only how fast
> we pass each other.
> And we change the speed
> by measuring it.

In the High Sierra
there are stretches of rock
valleys of pavement, moon mirrors,
where I saw no life.
Lower down,
squirrels lay in cold storage.
For six months of the year
Their blood is barely thawed.
Their hearts beat
four times a minute.

> The universe beats
> who knows how slow:
> lub dub, lub dub,
> matter to energy,
> energy to matter,
> over and out.

My genes are dreaming me,
dreaming my life
in their slow sleep:
Vishnu floats on the Cosmic Sea
dreaming the universe,
floats on the salt sea of my blood.
And I, a dream character, dream too,
asleep and awake.

Spirals

Life's wind whirls into us
through our fingertips,
say the Apache,
and leaves by the spin marks
in our footsoles.

Curved labyrinths
we chipped into cave walls—
still we paint them in playrooms,
doodle them on notepads.

They belong to old wells,
night seas of the mind
where spiders weave
in ever smaller curves,
and watchsprings of embryos
float, tucked in like galaxies.

Falling asleep,
or watching anesthesia
drip into my veins,
I see shell chambers,
water swirling down drains.

I meet her
in a chinked cabin
near timberline.
I wait in the second room,
a corner behind curtains.
She stands behind a secret door
I open when I am ready.

She resembles
other women I have known,
women with blue eyes
and short gray hair
who made music or paintings
or taught existentialism
standing with one foot on a chair.

But she wears deerskin,
and cloth of wild goats' wool;
thick spun shirt,
leather leggings,
soft boots shaped by her feet.
Her hooded cape hangs to her knees.
Her woven belt
has a silver crescent clasp.

She steps into the room.
Her mouth splits into a smile.
We hug each other and sit on the bed.
We speak earnestly
without words.
She gives me a page of poems
before I let her go.

Arachne

She was a weaver.
What she made was too perfect
for the gods to bear.
They were jealous, like her teachers.
They ripped her cloth.
She hanged herself.
They turned her into a spider.

I see spiders everywhere:
hanging dead in their cobwebs,
racing for cover across the floor.
Last night
one floated past me on the bathwater
and here's another,
pale and careful,
climbing over warp ties on my loom.
They're harmless,
but they distract me

and I make mistakes.

Fill up a bone bowl
with our eyes and tongues,
cut off our noses, ears,
our hands,
we will still find words.
They will crawl out,
drop from us like sweat,
You will know them
by their colors.

There are voices:
we repeat what we hear.
We stand in the great hall
with staffs in our hands, chanting
after you have feasted;
minstrels
reeling on the stoned road
a little crazy with hunger.

Casting Out

I am the masked executioner.
My eyes are hidden
behind familiar faces.
I am the hooded axe carrier.
I drive stakes
through the hearts of your demons.

All the monsters you fear,
blurry hulks in the doorway,
tiny green eyes
in your basement rooms,
are waiting to greet you.
Buzzards silently circling,
gathering, perching like gargoyles,
want to break into song.

Violet mushrooms are not poisonous
when you taste them
in small measures—
your blood carries antidotes
like slicks of oil,
peacock feathers drifting on darkness.

When the power fails,
all over the city
candles burn
with clean flames.

The underground ones
dwell in chasms below bridges.
Sometimes
they rest at the bottoms of wells,
swimming hidden rivers
from one to the next.
They overhear desperate wives
numbed by scorn,
broken freedom fighters,
neglected poets,
and they croon: let yourself fall.
                 Falling becomes flying.
                 The only way out is through.

The underground ones keep treasure.
They require all seekers
to give up words,
to move in a trance.
Then they say: to find what you want
                 you must know what it is
                 if only by what it isn't.

When you think you are ready
wait beside mounded earth
in the dark of the moon.
They gather in such places,
the fugitive remnant.
They may tolerate your confession;
they will leave when you lie.

Islanders

Most of our villages
are under water.
At low tide we can walk
to their ruins; at high tide
we tie rowboats to our doorknobs.
Those breakers out past the surfline
are beating on an old church steeple—
the pulpit floated ashore
in my grandmother's time.

South of here the storms took
a whole city in one night.
They say once a year it rises,
shines like a fleet of ghost ships;
children can see it
and the twice-born.

Our houses seem built to the ground
but they are attics on stilts,
crowsnests with skirts.
We climb up when the walls
wash away; we keep
our coffins there. They float.

When I Consider

julie king

Origins

I. In the blue north of night
    Earth Mother self-sowed.

    In yellow morning
    she gave birth to all things.
    All creatures slipped between her knees,
    among them our mothers,
    tilling the fields,
    and our fathers, husbandmen.

    Green of summer afternoon was theirs
    also red harvest nightfall,
    good death rattling seeds in its throat.

    Shadow and light moved together
    sharing the moon's face.

    The giant serpent shed its skins
    and slid peacefully in the deep.

II. In the heat of day
    the sons of Earth went mad.
    They denied their mother,
    called her harlot and devil.
    In fury, they brought fire and sword.

    Light was severed from darkness;
    all shadows, secrets, mysteries
    fled before the proud heat
    of the constant, withering sun.

    Our fathers cursed the giant snake.
    With their feet they broke its back
    and there was fear.

III. One of themselves they raised as god.
They claimed nothing else was holy.
They claimed their god made people
out of spit and dust.

Still we hear the deeper song:

The dust below their feet,
the rock beneath castles of reason,
the soil, the earth, is alive,
breathing,
beginning to shift.

When I Consider

I come closest to believing in God
the Father, Yahweh, Jehovah, Allah,
I come closest to believing God is male
when I consider the pain of women.

The book of police photographs
passed around at the meeting on rape:
I didn't close it fast enough,
the dead women float on my retina,
I see them on this paper
like watermarks

and behind the newspaper portraits
of those who would call me murderer
I see the one abandoned by the abortionist
face down in her blood on the kitchen floor.

Eve was expelled from the garden
because she knew too much.
Vengeance is mine, saith the Lord.

Fear

When I first heard he was coming after me
I locked my door and hid in the neighbors' kitchen.
They were surprised to find me there next morning
but they said I could stay, and I did, until
I saw him standing under the window, grinning
one afternoon just as I was pulling the shade.
Next I hung myself on a nail in the back fence
where the snow blew into a pile that covered around.
But my head stuck out, he could see my head,
so instead I crawled into the freezer chest,
under the beer, and arranged the icecubes
so no one could tell. (I spied him beating the snow,
swearing at the fence and the empty nail.)
Now I live in a tent, and I move it every day.

julie king

What shall I do with him?
They'll never believe it was self-defense.
I'll chop up his liver with chicken wings
and serve it to my mother.
Wednesday the trashman will take the paper bags;
if a tooth falls out I'll pound it into powder
with a hammer, on the cement doorstep
while the truck rolls south away.
(But what if they open the bags at the dump
and trace it all back to my address?)
After they're loose, his bones will fit
into one of the navy trunks in the bedroom,
and I'll bury it in a pet cemetery.
(But what if they dig it up after I go
because there's too much rattle for a collie,
and find his jaw and femur on the top?)
Something will distract the workers
while I slide him into the sear and glare
of a fir slash-burner; his ribcage will wilt
like troutbones thrown in the cooking fire.
(But what if they turn towards the smell
and see me running by the river?)
Best to compost him for the springtime.
(But what if I taste him in the radishes?)

Calling Out of a Wheelchair Painted Green

When you rolled me into the bright room
tight in white winding sheet
I pleaded to know why
and you ignored me.
The lumps are gone.
You sliced a groove between my legs
and it bleeds, it bleeds,
it splatters on the floor,
I wear a napkin like a codpiece
and a long sweater to cover the stain.

My legbones are bamboo splints;
the ends stick out my knees.
I try to pull them out, tugging,
and you restrain me.
You push me through a crowded hall
into a cave of masked faces.
Echoes suck behind my eyeballs.
Inside your fist
my skull collapses.

Here is her room.
It is full of voices.
They shout out of the walls
like a lynch mob.
The bed spins.
There is no light.

When she breaks
we note the elapsed time.
It's easy to alter the room
after she's passed out.
These filters slide on the windows.
This dial varies
the ringing in her ears.

If she tries to make sense of things
make the punishment random.
Or if she believes
her behavior is moral.
Here is the record book.
Be careful with the key.
I'm going to grab some lunch.
Have a good time.

After the wedding he watched basketball
on the motel TV, hunched in underwear
at the foot of the bed. She sat at the head,
against the wall, fingering rosebud buttons
on the obvious white chiffon nightgown
her mother gave her for the occasion.
It wasn't that he hadn't told her about the game.
It wasn't that she expected any joy.
Years later, before she asked for the divorce
they used to laugh and tell their friends about it,
how reasonable it was, unsentimental,
convenient, realistic, and urbane.
She never forgave him; he never apologized.

A Survivor Looks Back

I don't remember now just how the cold came;
a fog crept in behind when I wasn't looking
and slowly sifted snow into my mind.
I don't recall now when it was the tide moved,
but I turned around and the room was under water.
So I went to bed with my head stuffed full of cotton—
it was easier to sleep than try to breathe.
I was still alive: I burned my hand each morning,
sliced fingers on the breadboard every night.
I lost my wedding ring and bought another.
I stored my anger steaming on dry ice.

Water Rising

Because you love it, babe
I hate the sea.
The noise of surf seething,
slapping rocks
sets my jaw
and the spray makes all my hairs
writhe and stand.

You think you are a sunny pool
lined with anemones and grass

but you are shut up
at the end of a mucky tunnel
closed clam
and reaching for you
I cut my hand.

There is a place in the world
where women charged with witchery
were bound to a post
driven into the sand;
if they drowned, they were innocent.

I can see you on shore, watching,
either way
relieved.

Among the Malekulans

Among the Malekulans
men breed pigs for sacrifice
in status ceremonies.

They say these replace humans.

But now and then
a personage seeking the highest crown
offers a child,

a bastard bred for the purpose,
kept healthy, given
bounteous affection,

ignorant of the reasons.

Such a sacrifice is a feat as great
as can be expected in heaven or on earth.
It gives the celebrant much power.

Beware if your father favors you.

Blood Moon: A Month of Spotting

Red crysanthemums.
Albino eyes.
Footprints from a wine press.
Silent fireworks
blowing into dandelions,
magenta, cerise,
burgundy.
The rose window
in a cathedral
spinning apart
or color stills
of a nuclear explosion
from planes
directly above ground zero.
A fuchsia butterfly
drying its wings.
A bed of coals.

You Find Out What You Have to Do, And Then You Do It.

Whenever there was a crisis in the collective
Stephanie made tea.
The day we came home with news about Cambodia
she put the kettle on
and we sat crosslegged on the floor
breathing despair and sassafras steam.

I can remember when I was a kid if somebody died
my mother cooked a casserole and took it to the
family. She scotch taped instructions for how to
reheat it to the lid of the glass dish and printed
our name on a piece of adhesive tape and stuck that
to the bottom. A few days later it would come back,
someone would bring the dish over and speak a few
quiet words or we'd find it on the doormat when
we got home from town. It would be washed and we
could see the adhesive tape through the bottom.
I wondered how people could eat at a time like that
and my mother said those who are left alive have to
go on living.

We were on our way to town
the day the bombs came.
We saw the buildings fall,
slowly, like tall trees
and then their thunder slapped our ears.
We turned around for home.
Everywhere was burning,
people crying on each other,
animals dead in the street.
There was no fire in our house
but half of it was flat.
Some of it was blown away.
The men stood and talked
while we women swept up the kitchen floor
and picked rice and beans out of the shattered glass

and stretched tarpaulins where the roof had been.
The men discussed how to protect our water rights
from desperate neighbors.
We cooked the rice and beans.

I. First, anger.
   Then fear.
   He comforts me. Would it look like him?
      Does he want it
      would he say so if he did?

   Life insists.
   Red mushroom in my belly:
      already it drains me,
      feeds off my body,
      swells my breasts, they fill.

* * *

On the bus I see women,
wonder how many of us are two.
Does it show in my face?

* * *

Jars at the medical school
like a shelf of home-canned fish.
I don't remember
the one that lived five weeks.

When would it be born? October.
But it won't be born.
      Years from now I'll figure back
      how old it would have been.

* * *

I smile with the secret
and then I cry and beat the air with my fists.

The magazine waiting in the mailbox
carries on its cover a mother nursing her child.

Clothes rasp my nipples.
All day my nose wrinkles with nausea,
only cottage cheese, yogurt, oranges, peppermint tea.

I tell my friends.
They respond in their colors.

II. Waking, a flash dream: disaster.
        I am a refugee, wandering and begging,
        my belly growing. Weaker, weaker.

    Vision of a baby, naked, helpless,
        waving its arms and crying.

* * *

Somewhere I read that the Dakota people
before they killed,
apologized to the spirit of the animal.
And they asked its forgiveness afterwards.
Then they were absolved and could go on.

* * *

She asks: have you considered having the child?

I tighten: I must pay homage to its spirit
            but I know what I have to do.
            I have to travel light,
            another soul would be too heavy.

That's selfish.

So be it.

* * *

I cry hard sobs in the darkness,
        trapped, sick, weak.
He tells me crying is healthy.
I hear him but it's hard to believe.

I thought this would be simple,
        "just an office procedure."
I am not cool or stoical or steely or detached
        like I thought I would be
        like I thought I was supposed to be.

III. February 15: Susan Anthony's birthday.
Waiting to go to the clinic.
They said my stomach must be empty.
I have no desire to fill it.
I sleep, drink peppermint tea.
Wash my hair.

* * *

I will read the autobiography of Margaret Sanger.

Women have been doing this
for as long as there have been women,
handing down the wisdom,
dying for it.
Tansy. Lobelia.

Anne found her mother's knitting needle
in the bathroom
        before she was old enough
        to know why it was there
        but she knew why it was there.
Sharon went to Mexico in secret
        lay under the hands of a doctor

who would never see her again,
would deny he had ever seen her.
Melanie threw herself down the library stairs
when her period was late.
Up in the stacks she paged biology books
looking for symptoms.
Finally she loaded her arms with books
so she couldn't break her fall,
took a breath
and walked into space.
No one knew why. The college saw to it
that abrasive strips were installed on
every step, all over campus, to prevent
such accidents from happening.

We find a way.

* * *

Stirrings: race memory? sea surges.
I am fertile.
Simone de Beauvoir wrote of the resentment:
I am asked to bow before the Species.
My choice is irrelevant.
The deaf force uses me,
does not hear NO
does not understand NO.

I take matters into my own hands.

* * *

Pain down a tunnel
registers as burning,
fire on the end of a fishhook.

* * *

Home, lying under a blanket.
Small blood slips out of me into a pad.

I have been swimming hard for a long time.
Cramps.

Sea anemone floating in the measuring cup,
        white and pink, my body made it.
My confused body, shutting down:
        Plan B terminated,
        return to Plan A,
        rest.
Efficient, thorough, straightforward body,
making a flower until the flower was picked.

All over.
I am
                one
again.

Hundreds of us are leaving the building together
chanting and singing
and walking slowly, joyfully in the streets
beckoning to others to leave their work,
leave their husbands and fathers,
and come with us.
The procession is loving,
we have arms around each other,
we sing softly, moving with joy,
but with purpose.
It is not a parade,
there is no band or confetti, no drums,
only the sound of steady feet on the stones,
wearing them smooth.

Love Poem

I've learned from making wine
and watching gardens
there are things we cannot hurry
if we want to taste them ripe,
and sweet, and natural.
Today the vines leaned heavy
and our glasses sat full.
Sometime in our lives
I want to lie and hold you;
but we'll drink that wine
when the thirst comes.

I. Three of us at lunch together,
   I sat beside you in the cafe.
   You ate gratefully,
   rolled the cup rim along your lip.
   I wondered
   if you like drinking from straws
   or out of a bottle's mouth,
   I didn't know
   whether I could risk asking:
   do you melt custard on your tongue
   suck spaghetti noodles
   lick honey from spoons?

II. Waiting for you,
    mouthfuls of tea
    taste like champagne.
    Your voice on the phone
    was muffled, rounded,
    moved with pressure
    over my breasts.
    Night came on
    and I left the house dark.
    I'm standing in the kitchen
    watching for your headlights,
    my mouth hot and wet,
    my eyes strained wide,
    writing these words
    on the back of an envelope.

III. My nipples change like the moon.
     Since I heard tides in your earshell
     somewhere in my blood the sea moves.

Tonight the rain smells of oysters.
I roll a pearl with my tongue.

How long before you touched me
did I feel your hands?

To Susan: Written in Grass

Soft in the breathing, you lie knees loose,
breasts slide each down a rib to the floor.
Tucked into an egg, I roll where you reach me;
your reaping fingers glide through my hairs,
blades in a grainfield, each stalk
bending and returning, in the moving
making patterns with the others.
I wonder, with what's left of thinking,
if the earth feels her fields sway
and trembles with the living roots
in her thin scalp, when the wind touches.

Uncovered, in June music
we lie near the window
where a blue streetlight
silvers apple boughs
and the thickening grass
carries its rays lightly
on bladetips, film of snow.

With a blink, I see
leafless ribs rattling,
frost on the sidewalk
and suddenly behind your cheek,
hollow bone.

I cannot melt into summer
for noticing the blossoms fall.
Always from two steps away
I watch myself loving.

I wanted to take a picture of the garden
on summer solstice.
I counted twenty-nine kinds of flowers
from orange crepe poppies, shasta daisies,
a single saucer-wide peony
and rockets of foxglove
to tiny horehound, chamomile,
peas and tomatoes.
I wanted a picture of the garden
before this wind and rain beat it down.

And I wanted you in the picture,
maybe kneeling in the strawberries,
in the bed you dug and mulched
or under the fruit trees you pruned.
But somehow you were never home
when the sun was shining.

It doesn't matter.
I can see it all in my mind,
we're spared the cost of the film.
Summer comes again.
Still, all summers aren't the same,
nor gardens, nor lovers.
Now that the nights are longer
I'd like to have something that lasts,
something I could hold in my hand.

I. Many subtle roots of a great tree
   influence the earth
   without passion for control,
   simply by growing.

   One must either cut the tree
   or walk far away
   before planting gardens.

II. Old cultists were satisfied
    leaving gifts under the branches.
    I am profane.
    I crave a palpable sign.

    If this tree houses a spirit,
    let her bend and caress me.
    Otherwise I leave nothing of myself
    for strangers to steal.

Kiln Firing

It was meant
that I should love you with fire
guess the shape of your body
in the heat of my empty palms
bury my head
in the incense of your clothing
your face somewhere above me
warm and distant as the sun.

Now it is meant (I said)
that I should love you with water.
I found myself standing
over hissing coals,
a bowl in my hand.
I must make sure the fire is out.
I must make certain it is dead.
I have learned from it all I can.

Your power
pulled me to you yesterday—
its touch is strongest
from the center of wheels and clay.
I came to tell you about the ashes
and saw you shaping candlesticks,
dipping your fingers in gray water,
splattering water on the floor, my feet,
making handles for carrying flame.

This morning we slept in
and woke up slowly.
We nuzzled under warm blankets
and I rolled you in my mouth
before we got up for oatmeal pancakes
and honey, and apple juice.
A hole like a bushel basket
we filled with steamy compost
for the dense wood of a rhubarb root
heavy with buds waiting,
and we sowed some of each
of all the early vegetables.
When seeds grew dim in our palms
we stamped in for hot water,
soft flannel sweatpants,
the cat stretched by the floorheater,
sinking into twilight and kitchen chairs.

Over wine and brussels sprouts and cheese
we savored, counted over again
the best times we've made love:
the first night in my apartment,
New Years and the eighth floor snowstorm,
twice in the Arboretum
(when the impulse made us gasp and laugh)
and the time in your parents' camper.

> They were sleeping two feet away.
> We wanted each other with such ache
> I was so hot and slippery
> that as soon as we slid you inside
> we locked in spasms
> hardly moving, stifling groans,
> trying to make our breathing even.
> The next night we thought they didn't hear us
> not because we were so quiet

but because they were holding too.
Young affection budding near them
rushed them into their years of beds
maybe into early spring
when they made love in the guest bedroom
easy with trusting if their folks heard them
they'd be abashed, but not ashamed,
knowing the older pair would smile
in long recognition of good nights.

Loving
isn't from printed directions
with graphs and diagrams
and guaranteed results;
it's more like learning to dance
from the feel of the music:
I point to you
you point to me

we know

when we are ready

Song of the Washerwoman

Walking to the laundromat
forty pounds of clothes on my shoulders
all the oil and steam of our bodies
cold and solid in the cloth.

The laundromat is a hot breath;
I want to take my pants off
rub creams over my thighs
fall unconscious under the hum.

Walking home the bags are lighter.
Somewhere out of pipes our fumes rise.
When gods hold their hands over cities
they feel laundromats warm on their palms.

Love Poem

My eyes are frost marks
on a window pane.
A wave passes over my lips
when I speak.
A Kansas farmwoman's long nose,
square jaw and hands,
brow wide as Minerva's.
I have a gyroscope in my head.

My breasts are sometimes avocados,
sometimes oranges.
My mouth is like the moon.
In my chest hangs a birdcage;
a deep lake lines my belly.
My pubic hair: scrolls
on a vase,
moss on the forest floor.

From beneath my feet
my mirror sees
a fold in the earth
which opens into a ruby butterfly
with a garnet head.

Tight darnings spot my knees
and other scars stitch my chin,
my ankle, one wrist,
the bottom of my heel.
My legs reach the floor.
My toes are river pebbles in a row.

Soul Claiming

Alone on the road
crop-headed woman
bird-boned hitchhiker
spotting bad rides

carrying her past
like a photo in her pocket
choosing her future
by the highway signs

Mountain girl recluse
planting by the new moon
picking wild mushrooms
under veils of rain

gone for days
up near the glaciers
come back trembling
with fire in her veins.

Minstrel poet
singing for her supper
hungry for listeners
afraid of fame

painting her dreams
with her own bright bleeding
weaving robes for the spirits
changing her name.

julie king
DOUGLAS FIR